**COUNCIL** *on*
**FOREIGN**
**RELATIONS**

*Women and Foreign Policy*

I0005715

DISCUSSION PAPER

# Building Inclusive Economies
## How Women's Economic Advancement Promotes Sustainable Growth

Gayle Tzemach Lemmon
Rachel Vogelstein

June 2017

The Council on Foreign Relations (CFR) is an independent, nonpartisan membership organization, think tank, and publisher dedicated to being a resource for its members, government officials, business executives, journalists, educators and students, civic and religious leaders, and other interested citizens in order to help them better understand the world and the foreign policy choices facing the United States and other countries. Founded in 1921, CFR carries out its mission by maintaining a diverse membership, with special programs to promote interest and develop expertise in the next generation of foreign policy leaders; convening meetings at its headquarters in New York and in Washington, DC, and other cities where senior government officials, members of Congress, global leaders, and prominent thinkers come together with CFR members to discuss and debate major international issues; supporting a Studies Program that fosters independent research, enabling CFR scholars to produce articles, reports, and books and hold roundtables that analyze foreign policy issues and make concrete policy recommendations; publishing *Foreign Affairs*, the preeminent journal on international affairs and U.S. foreign policy; sponsoring Independent Task Forces that produce reports with both findings and policy prescriptions on the most important foreign policy topics; and providing up-to-date information and analysis about world events and American foreign policy on its website, CFR.org.

The Council on Foreign Relations takes no institutional positions on policy issues and has no affiliation with the U.S. government. All views expressed in its publications and on its website are the sole responsibility of the author or authors.

For further information about CFR or this paper, please write to the Council on Foreign Relations, 58 East 68th Street, New York, NY 10065, or call Communications at 212.434.9888. Visit CFR's website, www.cfr.org.

# Contents

# Acknowledgments

This report was produced under the guidance of CFR's advisory committee on economic inclusion and global growth, a distinguished group of experts from the government, multilateral organizations, and the private and public sectors. Over the past several months, members of this advisory committee have participated in meetings, reviewed drafts, and shared research and insights from their work. The report has been enhanced considerably by the expertise of this advisory group, and we are thankful for the members' participation. The views expressed here and any errors are our own.

A special acknowledgment is extended to James M. Lindsay, CFR's director of studies, for his support for this project. We are grateful to Patricia Dorff and Sumit Poudyal in Publications for their review of previous drafts and to Becky Allen, Anne Connell, and Lauren Hoffman for their assistance in the production of this paper. We also appreciate the expertise provided by Edwin Clarke in Liberia.

This report was published under the auspices of the Women and Foreign Policy program, and was made possible by the generous support of the William and Flora Hewlett Foundation.

Gayle Tzemach Lemmon
Rachel Vogelstein

# Introduction

The connection between women's economic participation and prosperity is undeniable. Over the past two decades, a growing number of international organizations and world leaders have recognized that the economic empowerment of women is critical to economic growth and stability. Analyses from the United Nations, International Monetary Fund (IMF), Organization for Economic Cooperation and Development (OECD), the World Bank, and other leading international institutions demonstrate the economic growth potential that follows from increasing women's labor force participation. Multilateral bodies such as the Group of Twenty (G20) and the Asia-Pacific Economic Cooperation (APEC) forum have ratified agreements to promote women in the economy as a means to stimulate growth, and governments from the Ivory Coast to Rwanda to Japan have adopted reforms to increase women's ability to contribute to their economies.

These developments have fueled mounting international recognition of the importance of women's economic advancement to poverty reduction and economic growth, manifested most notably in the landmark Sustainable Development Goals (SDGs) adopted at the United Nations in September 2015. The SDG framework not only emphasizes that addressing gender inequality in the economic sphere is critical to global progress but also prescribes action: for the first time ever, the global development agenda contains specific targets to improve women's economic participation, including equality in property ownership and inheritance and access to financial services, natural resources, and technology.

Yet despite this growing recognition, national and international economic leaders continue to make and measure policy in ways that undervalue women's work and do not capitalize on women's economic participation. Serious proposals to address critical barriers that limit women's economic contributions—from restrictions on the rights to work, own or inherit property, sign a contract, or open a bank account, to the absence of sufficient work-family policies—remain absent from mainstream economic policy discussions. The ways in which gender affects time use, human development, and access to assets and markets are too often ignored in policy dialogue. Women's work in the informal economy and inside the home is uncounted or undercounted. Structural and cultural barriers continue to inhibit women's participation in higher-wage sectors and occupations, and gender wage gaps persist everywhere in the world.

As nations struggle to emerge from a global economic slowdown, new strategies to jumpstart growth are sorely needed—and the economic potential of 50 percent of the world's population can no longer be overlooked. Suffocated opportunity hinders both global growth and stability. Given the strong evidence of the returns on women's economic inclusion, this issue merits a higher place on the U.S. economic and foreign policy agenda. The Donald J. Trump administration should build on recent reforms to promote inclusive economies and launch an effort to address legal barriers to women's economic participation; increase access to capital, especially among small- and medium-sized enterprises; catalyze investment in women; promote technology and innovation; and support research and data collection in this area. These steps will help boost prosperity, reduce poverty, grow economies, and promote U.S. interests in global stability.

# The Case for Women's Economic Inclusion

Although the gender gap in global employment continues to stagnate (see figure 1), an overwhelming body of evidence confirms that the economic benefits of promoting women's economic inclusion around the world are substantial. Empirical evidence indicates that enabling women to contribute can boost economies in four ways: higher macroeconomic growth, more favorable development outcomes, greater economic diversification, and lower levels of income inequality.

## MACROECONOMIC GAINS

Increasing women's economic participation offers the potential for significant macroeconomic gains, in both developing and developed economies. The World Economic Forum's Gender Gap Report has established a negative correlation between gender gaps—measured in the areas of health, education, economy, and politics—and overall economic productivity. Recent analyses suggest that the economic growth potential of closing these gaps and advancing women's economic equality is substantial. A 2016 McKinsey Global Institute report found that advancing women's equality could add up to $12 trillion—or 11 percent—to global gross domestic product (GDP) by 2025 in a "best in region" scenario, in which countries match the rate of improvement of the fastest-improving country in their region. A "full potential" scenario, in which women play fully equal roles in labor markets, could add a staggering $28 trillion—or 26 percent—to global GDP by 2025. This represents a net economic effect roughly equivalent to the size of combined Chinese and U.S. economies.[1]

Increasing women's economic participation would produce gains in nations of all income levels but most significantly in emerging economies. Data from the International Labor Organization (ILO) confirms

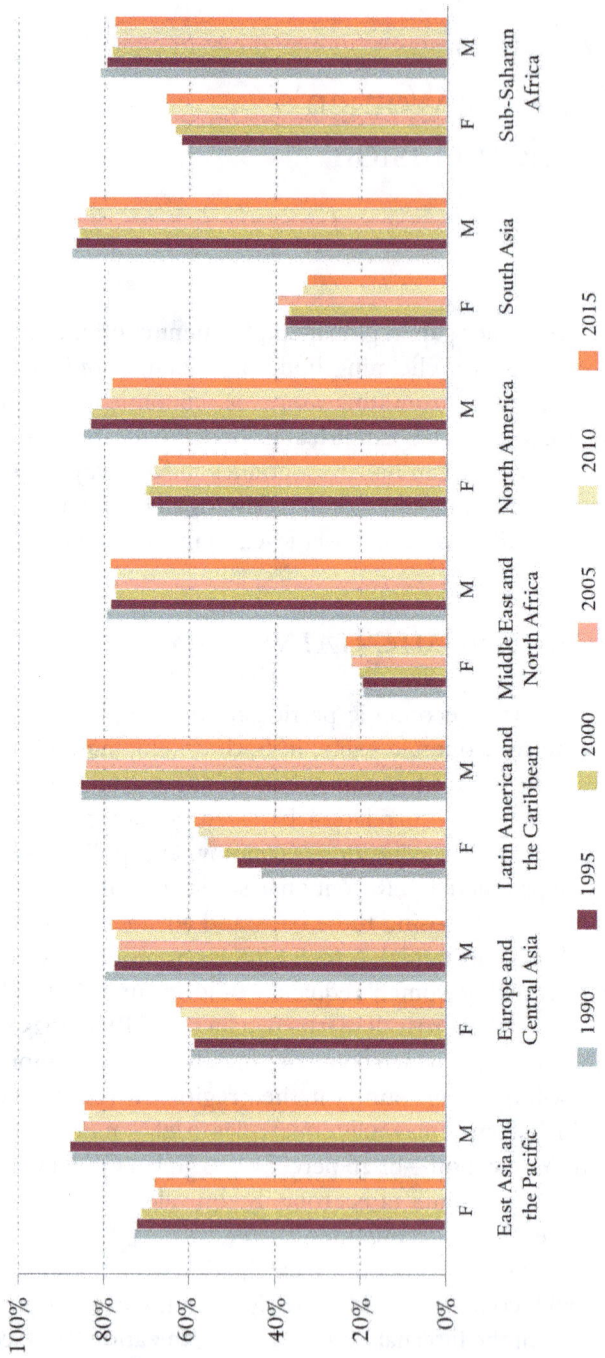

FIGURE 1. GENDER GAP IN GLOBAL LABOR FORCE PARTICIPATION

*Source:* World Bank.

that 94 percent of the estimated 865 million women worldwide who face significant barriers to full economic contribution live in developing nations. Studies conducted by the IMF also find the strongest correlation between advancement in gender equality and economic growth in low-income countries. For example, while closing the gender gap in labor force participation in the United States could boost GDP by an estimated 5 percent, gains in lower-income countries such as Egypt could be as high as 34 percent.[2] Analyses show that improving women's economic participation would produce the greatest regional gains in Latin America and South Asia, with India poised to make the largest economic improvement in the world.[3]

Increasing women's economic participation also produces macroeconomic benefits by mitigating demographic challenges. In rapidly aging nations, growing the share of women in the workplace can counter the deleterious economic effects of a shrinking workforce. In light of this evidence, some world leaders have taken steps to promote women's economic empowerment as a tool to mitigate demographic headwinds: in Japan, for instance, Prime Minister Shinzo Abe has incorporated "womenomics" as a core pillar of the nation's growth strategy, introducing a range of policies that includes legislation to expand childcare and to eliminate the tax deduction for dependent spouses. While challenges remain, these changes have contributed to a spike in female labor force participation in Japan, which reached a record 66 percent in just three years, while the national unemployment rate has fallen to a historic low.[4] Other nations with aging or declining populations—including Germany, South Korea, and Nordic countries—have also recognized the macroeconomic benefits of women's economic inclusion.[5]

## COUNTRY PROFILE: INDIA

In terms of net monetary gains, India stands to benefit more from women's economic empowerment and inclusion than any other nation in the world. Recognizing this growth potential, the government has introduced reforms to national economic policies to reflect how gender affects time use and access to assets and markets. For example, the government enacted an expansive worker protection program—the Mahatma Gandhi National Rural Employment Guarantee Act—which requires equal wages for men and women and includes provisions for childcare at worksites. In addition, in March 2017, India enacted a federal law mandating that all employers offer twenty-six weeks of paid maternity leave.

India has also led the way with self-help groups (SHGs), which are savings and credit association groups that manage and lend accumulated savings to their members.[6] These SHGs exist across the country and consist of groups of women lending to one another. With more than eight million SHGs across India, the Indian government is now using SHGs as a delivery channel for government services aimed at women. These efforts should be bolstered by initiatives to help women transition from the micro-economy to lead small- and medium-sized businesses, which have been shown to fuel economic growth.

India has also taken steps to advance women's financial inclusion through its Aadhaar program, the largest national identification initiative undertaken anywhere in the world. More than 99 percent of adults are now covered by Aadhaar, which relies on fingerprints and iris scans to create a national identity database. Women can open bank accounts using biometric information that tells financial institutions who they are. Thus, India has created a digital identification technique that has coincided with the digitization of banking and that makes "last mile" banking possible, especially for women, because a biometric method of identification makes it almost impossible for men to unilaterally access money in their wives' bank accounts and potentially spend it on non-household items.

Despite these efforts, however, an overwhelming—and growing—majority of Indian women work outside the formal economy and therefore fall outside government protection. Current estimates place India's rate of female participation in the formal labor force at only 30 percent—among the lowest in developing nations—a rate that has actually declined over the past decade across education levels and in both urban and rural areas. The majority of Indian women instead work in the informal sector in jobs with limited social protections and low wages.[7] The concentration of women in the informal sector is not driven by legal barriers, as India has relatively few laws that impede women's economic participation and Indian women have equal rights to obtain jobs, sign contracts, and open bank accounts. Instead, according to the ILO, cultural barriers and occupational segregation play important roles in limiting women's economic potential, as women in India tend to be grouped in industries and occupations that have not seen employment or wage growth in recent years.[8]

Because women's informal labor in markets, service jobs, garment work, and handicraft manufacturing is not captured by official definitions of economic productivity, national analyses value women's contributions to the country's GDP at only 17 percent. According to the McKinsey Global Institute, women's underrepresentation in the formal economy leads to a lost opportunity of $2.9 trillion annually in India's GDP; conversely, closing gender-based disparities in employment could result in a remarkable 27 percent boost to the GDP.[9]

Interviews confirm that India needs policies that better support women workers and investment in services and skills training for informal laborers that would add value to their activities.[10] Women affiliated with BASIX (a livelihood promotion institution), the Self Employed Women's Association, and Ujjivan (a financial services provider to the economically active poor), for example, cite persistent cultural barriers and stigma about women's work as barriers to economic participation. They also argue for the need for further government efforts to train women, including those presently working in the informal economy, for industries and occupations that are experiencing growth. Private sector companies and nongovernmental organizations (NGOs), such as Walmart and the IKEA Foundation, attempt to fill many of these gaps for their employees by providing women with skills training and access to savings and credit, health care, and childcare, among other services. Yet the reach of such programs is limited and, as ILO findings confirm, market rigidity largely prevents many women in the informal sector from transitioning into the formal economy.

## LONG-TERM POVERTY REDUCTION

The economic inclusion of women also produces sustainable develop-ment gains by decreasing poverty across generations. Research shows that women who are economically productive are significantly more likely than their male counterparts to reinvest high proportions of earned income into the health, nutrition, and education of their chil-dren. This phenomenon creates a multiplier effect in which families and communities grow healthier, are better educated, and are more econom-ically stable over time. These trends in women's reinvestment suggest that women's employment is a critical tool for sustainable development; it has the potential to reduce not only poverty but also child and mater-nal mortality, improve health and nutrition, and increase educational attainment. These gains make families stronger and more resilient.

Other studies confirm that national GDP growth is enhanced when women exercise greater control over household resources. Such control materializes the fastest when women work and earn in the formal econ-omy, but it can also be encouraged by tools and technologies that expand women's financial decision-making power in the informal sector. In countries as varied as Brazil, China, India, South Africa, and the United Kingdom, when women are involved in decision-making about the allo-cation of household income—through control over their own earnings, cash transfers, or mobile-technology initiatives targeting women—chil-dren and families benefit through increased household economic resil-ience and improved economic outcomes across generations.[11] Women have also been shown to make less risky financial investments and better savings decisions. One study of twenty semi-industrialized countries found that an aggregate domestic savings increase of roughly 15 percent-age points accompanies every 1 percentage point increase in the share of household income generated by women.[12] When women earn and save, families and communities become more financially stable; this only ben-efits countries seeking greater growth and prosperity for all their citizens.

## ECONOMIC DIVERSIFICATION

Policies to advance women's economic inclusion foster economic diversification, which is characterized by a number of different rev-enue streams and types of exports. Such diversification is crucial to producing more stable and sustainable growth, reducing volatility, and increasing resilience to external shocks.[13]

Advancing women's economic participation could accelerate and strengthen national efforts to diversify. Analyses from the World Bank and IMF find that gender inequality in economic participation decreases the variety of labor in the economy and the types of goods that countries produce and export, particularly in low-income and developing countries. This happens because gender gaps in opportunity constrain the potential pool of available human capital and gender gaps in the labor market impede innovation and decrease the efficiency of the labor force. When women and girls systematically lack access to the education and training necessary to enter a profession or when barriers prevent them from advancing within a workplace, entire industries suffer from a lack of access to the best talent and economies are more likely to be homogenous. Gender-inclusive policies, on the other hand, are strongly correlated with more broadly skilled labor forces that in turn help countries diversify economies. Indeed, economies that have advanced women's inclusion are more diversified and outperform those that have not.[14]

## REDUCTION IN INCOME INEQUALITY

Addressing gender inequality can also help reduce income inequality more broadly. This benefit is particularly timely today, as income disparities climb. While extreme poverty and income inequality among countries decreased in recent years, income inequality within developing countries increased 11 percent between 1990 and 2010.[15]

Improving women's economic inclusion could help address this challenge. A 2015 study conducted by the IMF using the United Nations' gender inequality index, which captures gender inequality in both outcomes (labor force participation gap and female seats in parliament) and opportunities (education gaps, maternal mortality, and adolescent fertility), found that gender equality is strongly associated with net income equality between the upper and lower earning brackets in a given society. This inequality occurs because gender inequality is most prevalent at the bottom of the economic ladder, exacerbating overall income inequality within a society. This earnings gap is further widened by the fact that poorer women around the world are dramatically more likely than affluent women to work in the informal sector, in which earnings are lower and risks are higher. Therefore, closing the gender gap in the economy could help narrow gaps between the rich and the poor inside a country, and between developed and developing countries.[16]

# Barriers to Women's Economic Participation

Despite strong evidence that women's economic inclusion has significant economic benefits, women in high-, middle-, and low-income countries continue to face a range of legal, structural, and cultural barriers that impede their full participation in the economy and undermine broader economic growth (see figure 2).

*FIGURE 2. LEGAL, STRUCTURAL, AND CULTURAL BARRIERS TO WOMEN'S ECONOMIC PARTICIPATION*

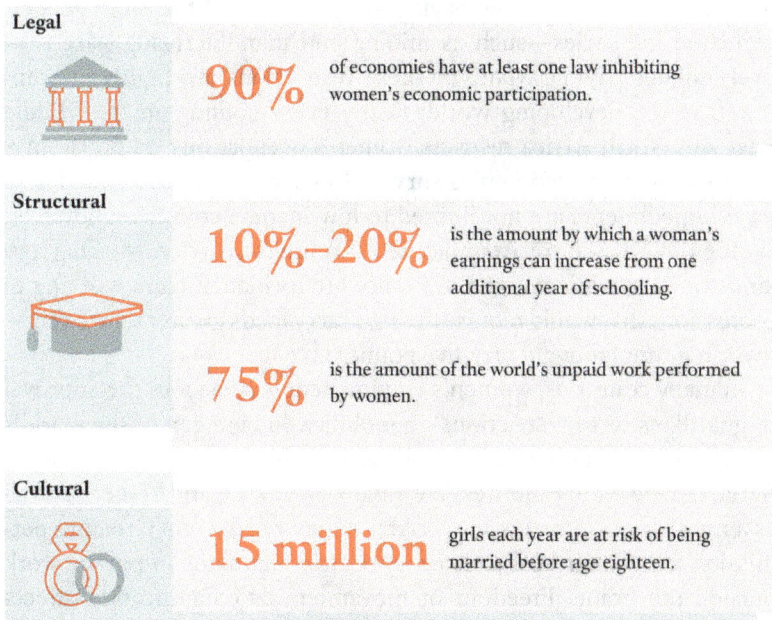

**Legal**

**90%** of economies have at least one law inhibiting women's economic participation.

**Structural**

**10%–20%** is the amount by which a woman's earnings can increase from one additional year of schooling.

**75%** is the amount of the world's unpaid work performed by women.

**Cultural**

**15 million** girls each year are at risk of being married before age eighteen.

*Source:* World Bank.

## LEGAL BARRIERS

According to the World Bank's *Women, Business, and the Law* report, an overwhelming 90 percent of the 173 economies surveyed have at least one legal policy that inhibits women's economic participation. Although some nations have made modest progress in reforming these laws in recent years, persistent gaps remain, and the pace of change is slow: today, a total of 943 gender-based disparities under the law still inhibit women's economic opportunity worldwide.[17] Legal barriers to women's economic participation include discrimination by job type and sector, restrictions on women's freedom and mobility, limitations on property and inheritance rights, lack of access to financial services, and insufficient legal protection from violence.

One hundred economies around the world limit the occupations and sectors in which women can be employed. These limits include restrictions on the hours women are permitted to work and the types of jobs they are allowed to hold. Not only do these barriers reduce the pool of qualified candidates but they also contribute to the confinement of women to low-paying jobs, as many of the more gender-regulated industries—such as mining and manufacturing—are relatively higher paying. Many of these restrictions are highly concentrated in the developing world: nearly every country in the Middle East and North Africa restricts women's occupations, as do twenty-eight of forty-one economies surveyed in sub-Saharan Africa. These legal impediments are not limited to low-income countries, however. Women in Russia, for example, face prohibitions from working 456 kinds of jobs, while women in France are forbidden from working in professions that would require them to carry loads greater than twenty-five kilograms (roughly fifty-five pounds).[18]

In many countries, women's employment is subject to the approval of guardians or to restrictions on mobility. In eighteen of the world's economies—including Bahrain, Iran, Jordan, Kuwait, Qatar, Sudan, Syria, United Arab Emirates, West Bank and Gaza, and Yemen, as well as a number of countries across Africa—married women require permission from their husbands or legal male guardians to pursue work outside the home. Freedom of movement also significantly affects women's economic participation: seventeen nations limit women's unaccompanied travel, which impedes access to economic resources, financial services, education, and other assets.

Women also face legal discrimination in asset and land ownership in many countries. Laws governing property ownership and inheritance permit discrimination against women, thus decreasing women's financial security and their household bargaining power as these limitations leave them with fewer assets in their names. A significant proportion of countries in South Asia, sub-Saharan Africa, and the Middle East and North Africa, for example, do not provide equal inheritance rights to widows.[19] While some countries have community property regimes that afford women access to assets such as land, others give husbands the right to control joint property, which has been shown to depress women's access to bank accounts. Without equal access to assets, women's financial inclusion and ability to access credit is reduced. Agricultural output is also undermined by women's lack of property rights; female farmers are up to 30 percent less productive than male farmers because they have access to fewer resources.[20]

Women around the world face significant legal hurdles in establishing their national identities and passing on citizenship to their children, which also impedes their economic participation. In ten nations, married women require extra documentation—often a birth certificate—to obtain a national identification card, and in rural areas and among communities that have experienced migration or conflict, documentation can be particularly difficult to provide. Without proof of identity, women could be left unable to find employment, open a bank account, or receive credit. This lack of identification documents diminishes women's already limited chances to access small business loans.[21] In addition, twenty-two countries do not grant citizenship by descent through the mother only. This means that children born to foreign fathers or single mothers are not guaranteed public services such as education and health care, and could be unable to acquire the documentation needed to join the workforce.

Women's economic potential is further limited by insufficient protection against gender-based violence; this lack of protection means lower earnings and decreased productivity. For example, research conducted in Vietnam found that the cost of intimate partner violence equaled 3 percent of GDP due to related out-of-pocket health expenditures, missed income from the inability to attend work, and productivity loss.[22] In Peru, the costs of partner violence against women reach almost 4 percent of annual GDP.[23] Another study found that intimate partner violence results in productivity losses equal to at least 1 percent of GDP in Tanzania, and, on an individual level, results in a woman who has experienced such violence earning 60 percent less than a woman who has not.[24] Despite the significant human, social, and economic costs of violence against women, more than one-quarter of countries worldwide—particularly in sub-Saharan Africa and across the Middle East and North Africa—have no explicit laws to address and punish domestic violence.[25]

## COUNTRY PROFILE: LIBERIA

Liberia's significant strides toward gender equality, educational parity, and economic growth have not translated to equality in the country's workforce. The majority of Liberians work in the informal economy, and, as in countries around the world, women still compose the majority of these laborers: 74 percent of female workers in Liberia are informal laborers, and even among those with a university education, 41 percent of women work informally, compared to 24 percent of men. Research confirms that the most significant challenges faced by female informal workers, such as market sellers and street vendors, include lack of access to credit and banking services, limited financial literacy and business training, few social protection and childcare options, harassment from citizens as well as local authorities, and poor sanitation within marketplaces.[26]

To grow the economic potential of Liberian women, a number of multilateral organizations and local groups have worked to address these obstacles. The UN Women's Next Level Business Program for Market Women brings skills and financial literacy training to women in the marketplaces of Monrovia, providing free childcare as women participate in workshops to learn about budgeting principles for small businesses and how to open a bank account. Program participants suggest that trainings make a difference in their abilities to support their children; most women confirm that they work primarily to provide for their children and to enable their children's education. Christiana Miller, a cross-border trader who trained women in the Next Level program, stated that "women did not know how to do banking. We taught them record keeping and banking, which made a difference because before they were only using local village savings programs and the people who ran those could run away with their money. Now they will save for family welfare, for children, for school fees, for their health."

The National Petty Trader Union for women in the informal economy also established a partnership with the Central Bank of Liberia to create a credit facility for women traders to receive small-dollar loans. However, Comfort Doryon, a member of the union, cited persistent challenges even when women did have access to financial services and credit: pervasive harassment and corruption on the part of local authorities resulted in the confiscation of women's goods, which frequently forced women to borrow capital from other workers and made them unable to afford school fees. Doryon explained that "there was a lot of harassment from national police, city police—they would always come and take the street vendors' goods and they would lose everything. We worked on an agreement with local authorities on street vendors' behalf." Other street vendors and service-providing organizations highlighted the need for better government regulation and the creation of binding memoranda of understanding with local authorities. These policies have allowed women some level of protection to be able to seek help if harassed.

Officials in the Ministry of Gender, Children, and Social Protection suggest that the government is aware of such challenges and is prioritizing the development of policies to protect informal women workers as well as enable their transition to the formal economy. The government's concrete steps to implement worker protections include the June 2015 signing of the Decent Work Bill—the country's first labor law since the 1950s—to set basic standards for safe working environments and collective bargaining rights for workers in the informal sector. The measure also sought to provide workers in the formal and informal economies standard minimum wages (US$5.50 and US$3.50 per day respectively) and guaranteed paid leave.[27] While few experts see this as a far-reaching solution, given the dominance of the informal economy and women's over-representation in it, the law sets a standard for what constitutes a national minimum wage. The ministry has also worked to improve the working conditions and provide financial and childcare services to women in the informal economy. Julia Duncan-Cassell, minister of gender and development, cited women's lack of access to information as a central challenge, noting that the ministry aims to get information about available services into the hands of women employed in marketplaces. She said, "Many women are working in the informal sector, and a central part of our work is to see how we take them from the informal to the formal by adding value to the business they are doing . . . either through education, financial inclusion, or capacity building."

## STRUCTURAL BARRIERS

Structural barriers throughout women's lives, such as inequalities in access to education and training, women's concentration in the informal economy, and the gender gap in unpaid and care work, also inhibit economic productivity for women, their families, and their nations.[28]

While significant progress has been made in closing the gender gap in education at the primary school level, gaps persist in many regions at the secondary level, which is critical to preparation for and transition to the workforce. Although two-thirds of the world's countries have achieved complete gender parity in primary school enrollment, less than half have achieved parity in lower secondary enrollment, and even fewer—less than one-quarter—have reached parity in upper secondary enrollment.[29] Girls living in poverty or in rural areas, as well as those who have been displaced from their homes, face the greatest educational disadvantages.[30] These educational gaps undermine women's economic potential and reduce broader economic growth: one study suggests that low- and middle-income countries that fail to capitalize on the growth potential of equal educational opportunities for boys and girls at the secondary level miss out on nearly $100 billion per year in GDP. In India, for example, where only 40 percent of girls are enrolled in upper secondary school, the economy fails to capture $32.6 billion of economic growth due to inequalities in education alone.[31]

Women's economic productivity is also limited by their overrepresentation in the informal sector and low-wage work, for example, in small businesses and service trades, in markets, or as domestic laborers (see figure 3). While women's participation in the informal economy is often absent from official statistics and economic analyses, recent estimates suggest that the informal economy contributes between 25 and 40 percent of GDP in developing countries in Asia and Africa. Women's participation in the informal economy is particularly high in developing nations, with 86 percent of employed women located in the informal sector: in India and Indonesia, nearly 90 percent of non-agriculturally employed women work in the informal sector, and in countries including Benin, Chad, and Mali as many as 95 percent of female workers do. Informal workers enjoy few of the benefits or protections offered to those in the formal economy, receive lower wages, and are frequently subjected to environments with poor health and safety standards that are more vulnerable to market volatility, thereby limiting earnings and productivity. They are also more vulnerable to harassment, which threatens both their physical safety and earnings.

*FIGURE 3. SHARE OF MEN AND WOMEN IN VULNERABLE EMPLOYMENT BY REGION*

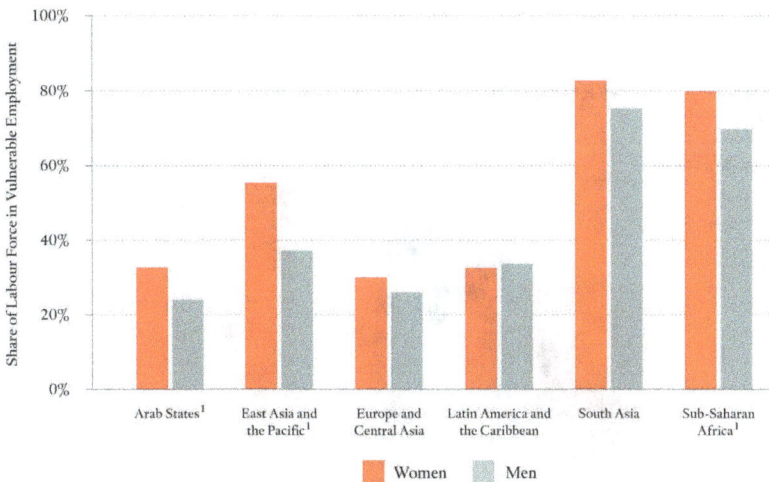

1. Data coverage is below the criteria used for regional aggregation.

*Source:* UN Development Program 2015 Human Development Report.

Women's economic participation is also reduced by the disproportionate burden of unpaid labor that falls on women around the world,
including domestic work such as cooking, cleaning, collecting water, and
caring for children, the sick, and the elderly (see figure 4). This unpaid
labor is essential for households and societies to function but is not
valued like paid work in the formal economy. Although recent estimates
show that women perform 75 percent of the world's unpaid work—effectively subsidizing the global economy—unpaid labor is barely captured
by standard economic modeling and remains unaddressed by national
economic policies.[32] This care work, although invisible, is invaluable to
the economy's success. Indeed, some economists suggest that the monetary value of women's unpaid work could amount to between 10 and 39
percent of global GDP.[33] Evidence shows a strong negative correlation
between time spent on unpaid work and female labor force participation: in countries where women spend an average of five hours per day or
more on unpaid work, only 50 percent of women are employed or seeking
employment in the formal sector. When that average decreases to three
hours per day on unpaid work, the women's labor force participation
rate rises to 60 percent.[34] Declines in women's time spent on unpaid care
work—through policies to improve childcare and eldercare services, for
example—correlate strongly with increases in women's economic activity and broader macroeconomic productivity.[35]

FIGURE 4. DISPROPORTIONATE BURDEN OF UNPAID WORK
ON WOMEN

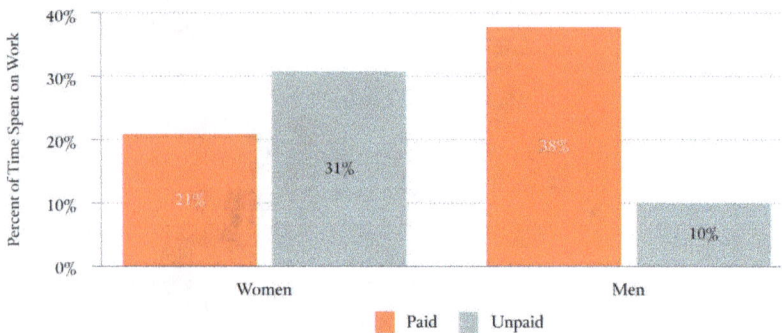

*Source:* UN Development Program 2015 Human Development Report.

## CULTURAL BARRIERS

Deeply entrenched cultural attitudes also limit women's lifelong employment opportunities and undermine economic growth. Gender gaps in opportunity begin early in life: for example, evidence confirms that in many societies school enrollment for boys is prioritized over that for girls when families cannot afford education for all children.[36] Cultural attitudes about gender roles and responsibilities also affect time use early on: girls between the ages of five and nine years worldwide spend a combined estimated 40 million more hours a day on household chores than boys, and girls aged ten to fourteen years spend 120 million more hours each day.[37] This shortens considerably the time girls have available for schooling and professional training, and can prevent families from prioritizing girls' education. The gender gap in children's time use is particularly prevalent in South Asia and the Middle East and North Africa, where female labor force participation is also low.[38] The opportunity gap emerges right at the start.

Marital norms are also deeply intertwined with women's economic opportunity. Child marriage, which affects one in three girls under the age of eighteen and one in nine under the age of fifteen, stunts educational achievement: research shows that early marriage often curtails education for young girls and adolescents and is correlated with illiteracy. Child marriage also impedes future employment potential: women married as children are often precluded from participating in the marketplace for years, which not only fuels dependency and poverty but also undermines economic growth. When childbearing starts during childhood, children born are poorer, less healthy, and less likely to be educated themselves. A recent joint study by the International Center for Research on Women and the World Bank suggests that curtailing child marriage would recapture earnings losses for women and girls as well as significantly increase per capita income at the household level and reduce public expenditures by putting girls back in the talent pool and reducing early motherhood. In Niger, for example, which has the world's highest child marriage prevalence rate, eliminating child marriage could translate to benefits of more than $25 billion by the year 2030.[39]

Even where educational attainment and the average age of marriage are high, cultural barriers surrounding the acceptability of women's work outside the home limit women's economic participation.

According to a new study by the ILO and Gallup, 34 percent of men and 30 percent of women worldwide still hold culturally rooted beliefs that it is unacceptable for women to hold jobs outside the home. In many contexts, this is due in part to concern about women's safety in public spaces and transport and the high prevalence of harassment of women and girls in the workplace. In light of these concerns, in many countries, men and women alike believe that women should not work outside the home. In North Africa, for example, where the gap between men's and women's views on women's work is largest, nearly half of men believe that women should not work outside the home.[40] Research from the Overseas Development Institute further suggests that attitudes about women's employment become increasingly negative during an economic downturn. Indeed, in many upper middle- and high-income countries, including China, Turkey, and South Korea, upward of 60 percent of people still believe that men are more entitled to jobs than women when jobs are scarce.[41] Across developed and developing countries, women frequently cite pervasive cultural barriers as one of the most significant obstacles to their economic participation.

## COUNTRY PROFILE: JAPAN

In the 1990s, Japan's female labor force participation rate was among the lowest in the developed world. In 2013, recognizing the power of women's economic participation to mitigate demographic challenges that threatened the Japanese economy, Prime Minister Shinzo Abe proposed "womenomics" as a core pillar of the nation's growth strategy.[42] Womenomics—a concept coined by Kathy Matsui, chief Japan strategist for Goldman Sachs—is based on research demonstrating that closing the gender gap in formal labor force participation would counter Japan's aging workforce and boost GDP by 13 to 15 percent.[43]

A range of Japanese policies in recent years, including legislation to expand childcare and eliminate a tax deduction for dependent spouses, contributed to a sharp rise in female labor force participation while national unemployment fell to a historic low.

Initially, the country's female labor force participation rate continued to lag behind that of peer nations, including other Group of Seven (G7) nations, and critics expressed skepticism that top-down political reforms would have a lasting benefit. But by 2016, female labor force participation had risen to 66 percent, surpassing that of the United States (64 percent).

Analysis of the success of womenomics finds areas of progress but also persistent challenges. Government policies to increase women's labor force participation have had little immediate effect on the strong cultural pressures that dissuade many Japanese women from staying in the workforce. Despite Japan's enactment of a fourteen-week paid leave policy—the standard suggested by the ILO—68 percent of women quit their jobs upon marriage or childbirth.[44] And although Japan offers one of the world's most generous gender-neutral parental leave policies, only 2 percent of fathers take any leave, compared with 83 percent of mothers.[45] Those women who do remain economically active are significantly more likely to pursue part-time or irregular work, a practice that hampers their career development; even in 2014, only 1 percent of executives in Japan's top twenty companies were women.[46] In light of these trends, the government has pledged to amplify policies to incentivize the use of gender-neutral leave policies, allow for flexible work environments, reform the tax code to reward dual earners, and combat workplace discrimination. The government has also committed to expand access to childcare, pledging the creation of half a million new spots by 2019.[47] These efforts should help Japan better capitalize on the growth potential of womenomics and, if successful, could provide a template for other nations facing comparable demographic challenges.

# Policy Considerations

Over the past several decades, as evidence linking women's economic advancement to macroeconomic growth has increased, women's economic participation has received greater attention from international economic institutions and multilateral organizations. Today, the World Bank contends that gender equality not only makes good economic sense but is central to the organization's development agenda. Its landmark 2012 World Development Report outlined strategies to enhance women's economic inclusion and productivity as a means to fuel growth. More recently, the IMF has put gender equality at the forefront of negotiations with member countries: for example, when the IMF's executive board approved a $12 billion loan to Egypt in 2016 to finance its budget deficit and bolster currency reserves, loan stipulations required a commitment to raise women's economic participation and improve transport safety for women.[48] Similar measures were introduced in an IMF-supported agreement with Jordan. Other multilateral bodies, from the G7 to the OECD, have made declarations and ratified agreements to promote women in the economy as a means to stimulate global growth. Important UN targets to advance women's economic inclusion were included under the SDG framework enacted in 2015, including equality in property ownership, inheritance, and access to financial services, natural resources, and technology. The following year, the UN secretary-general assembled the first High-Level Panel on Women's Economic Empowerment, which issued a comprehensive report identifying seven areas in need of investment to inspire progress toward the new development goals.[49] Additionally, more than 143 business leaders have signed on to the UN Women's Empowerment Principles, a guidance document resulting from collaboration between UN Women and the UN Global Compact that promotes win-win business standards that benefit businesses and economies.[50]

The United States has also increasingly recognized that advancing women's economic participation is critical to its strategic interests in global prosperity and stability, and has taken bipartisan steps to integrate women's economic empowerment into diplomacy and development efforts worldwide. In addition to exercising leadership in multilateral efforts to advance women's inclusion, consecutive presidential administrations have emphasized the importance of women's economic participation as part of U.S. foreign policy.

Under President George W. Bush's administration, gender equality and women's economic empowerment in the Middle East and South Asia were prioritized as tenets of aid to countries in post-conflict transition, most notably in Afghanistan.[51] In 2003, then Secretary of State Colin Powell announced the establishment of the U.S.-Middle East Partnership Initiative, which provided a framework and funding for the U.S. government to work with governments in Arab countries to expand economic, political, and educational opportunities, with a focus on empowerment and capacity-building for women.[52] In addition, the Office of International Women's Issues at the U.S. Department of State led bilateral initiatives to highlight the barriers women face in private enterprises, by, for example, hosting a U.S.-Finland business leaders' summit for fifty American and Baltic women chief executive officers to share best practices for including, promoting, and retaining women in the workforce.[53]

In 2009, President Barack Obama's administration established an Office of Global Women's Issues at the U.S. Department of State; that office led U.S. government efforts on women's economic empowerment and coordinated gender opportunity initiatives across the executive branch. In 2011, the United States hosted the first APEC ministerial meeting on Women in the Economy, in San Francisco, which led to historic commitments being made to advance women's economic participation in the subsequent signing of the APEC Leaders' Declaration on Women in the Economy. The United States worked with the other APEC members to establish the Women and the Economy Dashboard, a framework built to track and measure APEC's progress toward women's economic advancement goals.[54] And in 2014, the United States led efforts to work with leaders of G20 economies to set an ambitious and concrete target for women's labor force participation, establishing a goal of reducing the gender gap in participation rates in member countries by 25 percent by 2025.[55] The multilateral effort could bring an estimated 100 million additional women into the global workforce. In addition, the United States issued a strategy to promote women's economic empowerment and launched the Equal Futures Partnership, a multilateral initiative spearheaded by the White House to leverage U.S. leadership and spur other national commitments promoting women's economic and political participation.[56] Twenty-eight countries and the European Union have since signed on to the partnership.

The United States has also used innovative, goal-oriented foreign assistance programs to incentivize policies that advance women's economic participation. For example, in 2012, the Millennium Challenge Corporation (MCC), a U.S. development agency with a performance-based approach to economic growth, instituted new operational procedures focused on gender integration, including a "gender in the economy" indicator designed to measure and promote equality under the law. The indicator—which factors into MCC's determination of whether to invest in a given country—assesses women's abilities to obtain employment, register businesses and sign contracts, open bank accounts, choose a domicile, obtain passports and travel freely, pass on citizenship to offspring, and serve as heads of households.[57] MCC's performance-based approach has generated the so-called MCC effect, as some countries have enacted legal reforms to increase their competitiveness for U.S. investment: an MCC compact in Lesotho, for example, resulted in legal reform that ended women's status as minors under the law. In Mongolia, MCC supported a property rights project that increased the percentage of female landowners and prompted sex-disaggregated data collection by the government of land registration moving forward.[58]

## RECOMMENDATIONS FOR THE UNITED STATES

Despite recent efforts by the U.S. government and international institutions to advance women's economic inclusion, this imperative has not been as highly prioritized as other development and economic initiatives. Recent estimates find that investment in women's economic empowerment amounts to just 2 percent of overall aid from OECD countries, a remarkably low number given the high returns on women's economic participation. Economic policies that aim to reduce poverty or spur growth without focusing on the potential of women—and the legal, structural, and cultural barriers they face in making economic contributions—overlook a crucial growth opportunity and leave trillions of dollars of global GDP on the table.

By strengthening its focus on women's economic participation, the United States can improve the returns on its economic development efforts and promote cost efficiency by investing in a proven driver of economic growth. The Trump administration has expressed support for easing barriers to women's economic participation and, correspondingly, should take steps to grow the U.S. commitment to unlocking their economic potential. Even in an era of tightening budgets, Washington can reprogram existing economic development funding to promote women's economic empowerment as a tool to accelerate growth and reduce poverty. The United States could maximize its own financing by spearheading an effort to increase global support for women's economic participation and co-invest with partner governments, multilateral organizations, the private sector, and civil society. Such an effort would strengthen the effect of U.S. investments by promoting a shared infrastructure and reducing inefficiency. With its partners, the U.S. government should support legal reform through diplomatic efforts, increase women's access to capital and financial services, incentivize economic inclusion, promote technology and innovation, and support research and data collection. Washington can also lead by example and stimulate growth by implementing its commitment to leveling the economic playing field for women within the country.

### INCENTIVIZE LEGAL AND POLICY REFORM

The U.S. government should promote legal and policy reform to advance women's economic participation through its bilateral and multilateral relations. This is not just good policy; it is good economics. Washington can address constraints on female workers and entrepreneurs through bilateral investment treaties and trade agreements. When negotiating such agreements, officials should consider including stipulations to increase women's economic participation, improve women businessowners' access to supply chains, and support women workers.[59]

At the bilateral level, the United States should build on MCC's model to promote legal reform that levels the playing field for women, by providing incentives across U.S. foreign assistance programs to tackle legal barriers to women's economic participation. The United States also should promote policies to expand women's economic participation, including through vigorous enforcement of antidiscrimination and equal pay laws, childcare and eldercare support, paid family and medical leave programs that reach all workers, and tax reform that eliminates the penalization of dual-income families. Some of these policies have already proved effective in increasing women's labor force participation in other nations. For instance, when Morocco increased maternity leave from twelve to fourteen weeks, the nation saw an increase in the number of working mothers.[60] In addition, in countries where affordable and high-quality childcare is available, women's labor force participation rises. For example, as a result of a flagship government program in Chile, "Chile Crece Contigo" (Chile Grows With You), the number of public daycares and places for children under one year of age increased from seven hundred in March 2006 to more than four thousand by the end of 2009 and from fourteen thousand in 2005 to eighty-five thousand in March 2010. Early evaluations of the program suggest that it could increase the probability of Chilean mothers gaining employment by close to 15 percent.[61]

The United States also can use its influence on the multilateral stage to help eliminate legal barriers to women's economic inclusion and promote women's economic advancement. The United States should build on its landmark APEC Declaration on Women in the Economy by spearheading similar efforts in other regional bodies and leading the way for other countries to eliminate obstacles to women's participation. The United States has already expanded its focus on this issue at the G20, for example, by working with other major economies to address barriers to women's economic inclusion. The United States should support the extensive recommendations outlined in the communiqué presented to core negotiations during the 2017 Berlin G20 Summit, which included measures to strengthen women's economic empowerment, close the gender pay gap, promote microfinance opportunities in developing countries, and ensure women's representation in the boardroom.[62] Washington should also propose an annual review mechanism to track progress toward the Brisbane Summit goal of including 100 million more women in the labor force by 2025. U.S. officials should ensure that women are not relegated to microenterprises and instead incorporate women's ownership of small and medium enterprises (SMEs) into economic growth strategies. The United States should also support efforts at the IMF and other economic institutions to make legal and policy reform regarding women in the economy a precondition of investment and positive economic assessment, including, for example, the IMF's pilot program to integrate assessments of gender-inclusive economic policies into its national review processes in twenty nations.

## INCREASE WOMEN'S ACCESS
## TO CAPITAL AND FINANCIAL SERVICES

The U.S. government should expand its work through the Overseas Private Investment Corporation (OPIC) to narrow gender gaps in access to capital. Currently, OPIC partners with the International Finance Corporation and Goldman Sachs on a women entrepreneurs opportunity facility, with a goal of providing 100,000 women entrepreneurs access to capital and financial services. The United States should build on this program and others that focus on SMEs, including the Global Banking Alliance for Women, by supporting efforts to design and introduce financial products targeted to women. Some already exist, offering longer repayment plans, lower interest rates, and different collateral requirements, as well as leasing and factoring options, for women-owned businesses. Such businesses should be given focused financing through these channels, just as U.S. businesses are currently prioritized for OPIC financing.

The U.S. government should also work with Women's World Banking and partner banks to promote financial inclusion through mobile technology, incorporating lessons learned from the groundbreaking example set by the M-PESA mobile banking and financing service in Kenya, which catalyzed long-term poverty reduction and improved women's ability to save, invest, and work.[63] For example, the United States could lead efforts to extend to other nations the Nigerian Beta savings account model, in which female bank agents with mobile devices travel to markets to help women vendors set up and maintain bank accounts without having to leave their stalls. The accounts require neither documentation nor a minimum balance, thanks to Nigeria's tiered Know Your Customer (KYC) requirements, which have enabled Beta to reach 270,000 clients in Nigeria. Scaling this model to other countries would help close the gender gap in banking, enabling women to save both money and time otherwise spent traveling to a bank branch, and promoting women's savings and entrepreneurship. It also helps keep women safer by eliminating the need to carry cash while traveling from work to home.

## COUNTRY PROFILE: PERU

Peru illustrates how legal reforms can effectively drive an increase in female labor force participation and financial inclusion. During the 1990s, the country modified the customary laws—followed primarily in indigenous and rural communities—that limited women's legal rights to work, access banking and financial services, and own and inherit assets. Following the enactment of these reforms, women's formal labor force participation increased by 15 percent within a decade, and ensuing national growth has led to Peru today having one of the fastest growing economies in Latin America.[64]

Growth in female labor market participation continues but has tapered since the reforms of the 1990s, and gender gaps in economic participation remain widest in poor, rural, and indigenous communities. In the context of a shortage of formal employment and little national investment in production, many businesses continue to operate informally. Women who are unable to find jobs in the formal economy frequently head their own small and medium enterprises out of necessity, and about 70 percent of these business ventures are informal.[65] According to the IDB's WEVentureScope Index, because of the wide availability of capacity and skills training and relatively strong access to capital, Peru ranks as the second-best environment for female business owners and entrepreneurs across Latin America and the Caribbean.[66]

However, many women who run microenterprises face challenges in accessing formal financial institutions and achieving the financial literacy necessary to scale their businesses or bring them into the formal sector. Making the leap from micro- to small- and medium-sized businesses can be especially difficult for women due to a shortage of skills and capital. Women operating self-owned businesses in the informal economy are not covered by government policies to promote and protect women in the workforce and are more vulnerable to market risks. Government data shows that 60 percent of all women workers in the country continue to operate informally, with only 15 percent having health coverage, 4 percent enjoying retirement benefits, and few benefiting from the 2015 law that extended paid maternity leave from ninety to ninety-eight days.[67]

## CREATE AN ECONOMIC INCLUSION CHALLENGE FUND

The U.S. government should create a public-private fund to develop innovative approaches to improving women's economic participation. Such an initiative could build upon the U.S. government effort already underway, in collaboration with the World Bank, to create a financing facility to benefit female entrepreneurs globally. The U.S. government should expand this effort to leverage social impact bonds, results-based financing for governments, and co-investment with foundations and corporate philanthropies to support comprehensive programs to advance women's economic empowerment, including not only access to finance but also services such as literacy, legal, and business skills training. Promoting access to networks of buyers and suppliers and market linkage opportunities, both domestic and international, would further the goal of boosting women's economic participation and foster broader growth. In addition, the fund should support subsidized schools and childcare centers at marketplaces where large numbers of women work. This relatively inexpensive investment would simultaneously reduce the cost and travel time required for market women to ensure that children receive education and quality care and would offer more children access to education. The fund should also be used to assist governments in countries with high concentrations of women in the informal sector and low-wage work to promote transitions into the formal economy, where those pathways exist. For example, the fund could target tax breaks or enhanced access to financial services for companies that move women from the informal to the formal economy.

The United States should also partner with the private sector to expand recent efforts to source from women-owned businesses. For its part, the United States should amend its foreign assistance contracting and procurement policies to create incentives for contractors to hire women or women-owned businesses, modeled after domestic requirements that promote contract awards for U.S. businesses owned by women.[68] Similarly, the private sector could build upon existing commitments—such as the recent initiative announced by several Fortune 500 companies, including Walmart, ExxonMobil, and Coca-Cola—to boost women's economic participation by sourcing from women-owned businesses around the world.[69]

## PROMOTE TECHNOLOGY AND INNOVATION

The U.S. government should invest strategically in existing time-saving technologies for households in developing economies, including clean cookstoves, wells and pipe water, and electricity, and collaborate with the private sector to create and promote innovative approaches to reduce the burden of unpaid work on women and girls. Such technologies have proved to be effective in reducing the time required for unpaid household work and increasing female labor force participation. For example, the spread of electricity in rural South Africa decreased the time spent by women on unpaid care work and increased their labor force participation rate by 9 percent. Similarly, the female labor force participation rate increased in Pakistan when water sources were moved closer to women's homes.[70] Investment from the U.S. government and leading private sector companies in such time-saving technologies and infrastructure projects should be undertaken in concert with leaders on the ground and with the aim of building long-term technical capacities in emerging economies.

The U.S. government should also increase investment in programs that support women's entry into growing science, technology, engineering, mathematics (STEM) industries. For example, the Laboratoria initiative—which has locations in Peru, Mexico, and Chile, with expansion plans across the region—provides skills training to young women and is a leading source of female technological workers for private sector companies, with over one hundred and fifty companies in Latin America and the United States already hiring women through the program.[71] The United States could partner with the private sector to scale this model and bring it to other regions.

## SUPPORT RESEARCH AND DATA COLLECTION

Women's unpaid and informal work—which subsidize the global economy—are still largely absent from mainstream economic analysis. This has consequences, because what is not seen is not counted, and nobody invests in invisible things. The United States should lead an effort to help close this economic gender data gap by ensuring that all work—whether in the formal or informal sectors, paid or unpaid—is measured. Generating a more complete picture of women's work in the unpaid and the informal sectors also will help craft policies to facilitate women's inclusion in the formal economy.

The U.S. government should work with the ILO, the Bill and Melinda Gates Foundation, the National Transfer Accounts Project—which gathers global data on informal work—and other partners to lead comprehensive efforts to close the economic gender data gap and analyze women's unpaid care work and informal economy activity. To create an international baseline, data should conform to a common framework that enables comparability across countries. To that end, the U.S. government should support the implementation of the 2013 International Conference of Labor Statisticians resolution to amend international definitions of work and employment to better reflect gender considerations and informal sector work.[72] Household-level time-use surveys should collect sex-disaggregated data based on the following indicators: care for children, the elderly, and the sick; collection of fuel and water; household tasks; education; and time spent on leisure activities. Analysts and statisticians could then use the data collected in the time-use surveys to generate an accurate picture of women's work and measure the effect of women's contributions on GDP. This approach has been successfully employed by the National Institute of Geography and Statistics in Mexico, which valued unpaid labor from women at approximately 20 percent of GDP in 2012 and that from men at 6 percent.[73]

In addition, the United States should support data collection on women's financial inclusion. For example, the U.S. government could encourage banks to collect sex-disaggregated data on their client base, which would help identify gaps in access to finance and target financial products to women.

### LEAD BY EXAMPLE

The U.S. government should lead by example by developing domestic policies to advance women's economic participation at home, including through enforcement of U.S. antidiscrimination and equal pay laws, among them Title VII and the Equal Pay Act; expanded support for quality, affordable childcare and eldercare; tax reform to eliminate the penalization of dual-income families; and the development of a paid family-leave program, given that the United States is one of only nine countries in the world without such a policy. The Trump administration has already pledged to work with Congress to provide affordable and accessible childcare and paid family leave for new parents; it should act upon this commitment by advancing proposals on Capitol Hill, potentially as part of a tax reform package. Government leaders also should translate rhetorical support for equal pay into concrete reforms—such as pay transparency and anti-retaliation requirements—which could be accomplished through administrative or legislative means.

In addition, Washington should take steps to promote women's access to capital in the United States to address the shortfall in venture capital support for female entrepreneurs and grow women's small- and medium-sized businesses as a tool to boost economic growth. The administration could increase support for female entrepreneurs through the Small Business Administration and promote efforts by private sector leaders to source from women-led U.S. businesses through tax breaks and other incentives.

The U.S. government should also set an example with regard to trade agreements by committing to review existing and new trade agreements to evaluate potential effects on women and girls. Such reviews should include taking steps to ensure that agreements advance women's economic potential and ability to contribute to their economies. Special attention should be paid to trade liberalization, which could enhance market women's ability to sell their goods across borders but could also disadvantage women who have less mobility, access to technology, and skills than men. The U.S. government should support efforts to provide special training to women on cross-border trading, as UN Women has in Liberia, and should encourage partner governments to conduct their own gender assessments of trade agreements.

# Conclusion

Women represent a valuable economic reserve that has yet to be fully tapped. In a time of economic challenge, no economic talent or potential can be left on the sidelines. Strong evidence demonstrates that women's inclusion in the economy will advance U.S. interests in global prosperity, poverty reduction, and economic growth. Increasing women's economic participation would produce significant gains in nations of all income levels, which could total tens of trillions in global growth, thereby strengthening the U.S. economy and overall stability. To boost global GDP and capitalize on women's economic potential, efforts to eliminate the legal, structural, and cultural barriers to women's economic participation merit a higher place on the U.S. foreign policy agenda. Stymied opportunity is the opponent of global stability, and making the most of the entire talent pool—and the entire population— is in U.S. interests.

# Endnotes

1. McKinsey Global Institute, "How Advancing Women's Equality Can Add $12 Trillion to Global Growth," 2015, http://mckinsey.com/global-themes/employment-and-growth/how-advancing-womens-equality-can-add-12-trillion-to-global-growth.
2. Katrin Elborgh-Woytek et al., "Women, Work, and the Economy: Macroeconomic Gains from Gender Equity," International Monetary Fund (IMF), 2013, https://imf.org/external/pubs/ft/sdn/2013/sdn1310.pdf.
3. McKinsey Global Institute, "The Power of Parity: Advancing Women's Equality in India," 2015, http://mckinsey.com/global-themes/employment-and-growth/the-power-of-parity-advancing-womens-equality-in-india.
4. Elborgh-Woytek et al., 2013.
5. Yuko Kinoshita and Fang Guo, "IMF Survey: Nordic Lessons to Raise Female Labor Participation in NE Asia," 2015, http://imf.org/external/pubs/ft/survey/so/2015/car031615a.htm.
6. Ajay Tankha, "Self-Help Groups as Financial Intermediaries in India: Cost of Promotion, Sustainability, and Impact," 2002.
7. Piritta Sorsa et al., "Determinants of Low Female Labour Force Participation," Organization for Economic Cooperation and Development (OECD), 2015, http://www.oecd.org/officialdocuments/publicdisplaydocumentpdf/?cote=ECO/WKP(2015)25&docLanguage=En.
8. International Labor Organization (ILO), "India: Why is women's labour force participation dropping?," 2013, http://ilo.org/global/about-the-ilo/newsroom/news/WCMS_204762/lang--en/index.htm.
9. McKinsey Global Institute, "The Power of Parity."
10. Interviews conducted by Gayle Tzemach Lemmon in Bengaluru, Hyderabad, and New Delhi, India, March 6–10, 2017.
11. World Bank, "World Development Report 2012: Gender Equality and Development," 2012, https://openknowledge.worldbank.org/handle/10986/4391.
12. Hillary Rodham Clinton, "Remarks at the Asia Pacific Economic Cooperation Women and the Economy Summit," September 16, 2011, U.S. Department of State, https://2009-2017.state.gov/secretary/20092013clinton/rm/2011/09/172605.htm.
13. Rodney Ramcharan, "How Big Are the Benefits of Economic Diversification? Evidence from Earthquakes," IMF Working Paper, 2005, https://www.imf.org/external/pubs/cat/longres.aspx?sk=17985.0.
14. Romina Kazandjian et al., "Gender Equality and Economic Diversification," IMF Working Paper, 2016, http://imf.org/external/pubs/ft/wp/2016/wp16140.pdf.
15. "Goal 10: Reduce Inequality Within and Among Countries," United Nations, http://un.org/sustainabledevelopment/inequality.

16. Sonali Jain-Chandra, Kalpana Kochhar, and Monique Newiak, "Empowering Women, Tackling Income Inequality," 2015, https://blog-imfdirect.imf.org/2015/10/22/empowering-women-tackling-income-inequality.

17. World Bank, "Women, Business, and the Law 2016: Getting to Equal," 2016, http://wbl.worldbank.org/~/media/WBG/WBL/Documents/%20Reports/2016/Women-Business-and-the-Law-2016.pdf.

18. Ibid., 9.

19. Ibid., 12–13.

20. Leading economists at the IMF suggest that recent declines in commodity prices around the world and global predictions for stagnating commodity prices in the medium term should serve as powerful reminders for countries to diversify their production and export bases.

21. Recent scholarship confirms that reducing national income inequality produces significant economic benefits, with lower net income inequality associated with higher investment in physical and human capital, faster economic growth, resiliency to economic shocks and crises, and longer periods of growth. Reducing income inequality is also a security imperative, as evidence shows that failure to do so perpetuates cyclical poverty, increases morbidity and mortality rates, erodes social cohesion, and leads to higher rates of grievance against governments.

22. Natalie Duvvury et al., "Intimate Partner Violence: Economic Costs and Implications for Growth and Development," World Bank, 2013, http://documents.worldbank.org/curated/en/412091468337843649/pdf/825320WP0Intim00Box379862B00PUBLIC0.pdf.

23. GIZ, executive summary to "Violence Against Women and Its Financial Consequences for Businesses in Peru," 2014, https://giz.de/en/downloads/giz2014-0251en-violence-women-financial-consequences-peru.pdf.

24. Seema Vyas, "Estimating the Association Between Women's Earnings and Partner Violence: Evidence from the 2008-2009 Tanzania National Panel Survey," 2013, p. 20, https://openknowledge.worldbank.org/bitstream/handle/10986/16696/825350WP0Estim0379862B00PUBLIC0.pdf.pdf?sequence=1&isAllowed=y.

25. World Bank, 2016, 21–23.

26. UN Development Program (UNDP), "Advancing Economic Empowerment of Women: An Analysis from the Field," 2013, pp. 1–5, http://africa.undp.org/content/rba/en/home/library/reports/women-empowerment/advancing-economic-empowerment-of-women-in-africa.html.

27. Aeneas Chapinga Chuma, "Liberia's New Labor Law Commits to Decent Work," ILO, July 24, 2015, http://ilo.org/global/about-the-ilo/newsroom/news/WCMS_384403/lang--en/index.htm.

28. World Bank, "Gender at Work: A Companion to the World Development Report on Jobs," 2014, http://documents.worldbank.org/curated/en/884131468332686103/pdf/892730WP0Box3800report0Feb-02002014.pdf

29. UN Educational, Scientific, and Cultural Organization (UNESCO), "Gender Review: Creating Sustainable Futures for All," 2016, http://unesdoc.unesco.org/images/0024/002460/246045e.pdf.

30. Ibid.

31. Plan, "Paying the Price: The Economic Cost of Failing to Educate Girls," 2008, pp. 8–11, https://planusa.org/docs/PayingthePrice.pdf; UNESCO, 2016, 31.

32. UNDP, "Human Development Report 2016," pp. 105–133, http://hdr.undp.org/sites/default/files/chapter4.pdf.

33. UN Research Institute for Social Development, "UNRISD Research and Policy Brief 9," 2009, http://unrisd.org/80256B3C005BCCF9/httpNetITFramePDF?Rea dForm&parentunid=25697FE238192066C12576D4004CFE50&parentdoctype =brief&netitpath=80256B3C005BCCF9/(httpAuxPages)/25697FE238192066C1 2576D4004CFE50/$file/RPB9e.pdf.

34. Gaëlle Ferrant, Luca Maria Pesando, and Keiko Nowacka, "Unpaid Care Work: The Missing Link in the Analysis of Gender Gaps in Labor Outcomes," 2014, p. 5, https:// oecd.org/dev/development-gender/Unpaid_care_work.pdf.

35. Jerome De Henau et al., "Investing in the Care Economy: A Gender Analysis of Employment Stimulus in Seven OECD Countries," International Trade Union Confederation, 2016, http://ituc-csi.org/investing-in-the-care-economy; Ipek Ilkkaracan, Kijong Kim, and Tolga Kaya, "The Impact of Public Investment in Social Care Services on Employment, Gender Equality, and Poverty: The Turkish Case," Istanbul Technical University and the Levy Economics Institute of Bard College, 2015, http:// levyinstitute.org/pubs/rpr_8_15.pdf; OECD, "Gender and Sustainable Development: Maximizing the Economic, Social, and Environmental Role of Women," 2008, https://oecd.org/greengrowth/40881538.pdf; Sebastian Martines, Sophie Naudeau, and Vitor Pereira, "The Promise of Preschool in Africa: A Randomized Impact Evaluation of Early Childhood Development in Rural Mozambique," World Bank and Save the Children, February 2012, http://siteresources.worldbank.org/INTAFRICA /Resources/The_Promise_of_Preschool_in_Africa_ECD_REPORT.pdf.

36. UNICEF, "Goal: Promote Gender Equality and Empower Women," https://www.unicef .org/mdg/index_genderequality.htm.

37. UNICEF, "Girls Spend 160 Million More Hours Than Boys Doing Household Chores Everyday," news release, 2016, https://www.unicef.org/media/media_92884.html.

38. Ibid.

39. Costs of Child Marriage, "Economic Impacts of Child Marriage: Preliminary Findings From Analyses of Existing Data," 2015, http://costsofchildmarriage.org/publication /economic-impacts-child-marriage-preliminary-findings-analyses-existing-data.

40. Gallup and the ILO, "Towards a Better future for Women and Work: Voices of Women and Men," 2017, http://www.ilo.org/wcmsp5/groups/public/---dgreports/---dcomm /---publ/documents/publication/wcms_546256.pdf.

41. Pew Research Center, "Gender Equality Universally Embraced, But Inequalities Acknowledged," 2010, http://pewglobal.org/2010/07/01; Abigail Hunt and Emma Samman, "Women's Economic Empowerment: Navigating Enablers and Constraints," Overseas Development Institute, 2016, https://www.odi.org/sites/odi.org.uk/files /resource-documents/10683.pdf.

42. Kathy Matsui, "'Womenomics' Continues as a Work in Progress," *Japan Times*, September 16, 2016, http://japantimes.co.jp/news/2016/05/25/business/economy-business /womenomics-continues-work-progress/#.WOJ0Rm_yu70.

43. Goldman Sachs, "Womenomics 3.0: The Time Is Now," 2010, http://goldmansachs .com/our-thinking/investing-in-women/bios-pdfs/womenomics3_the_time_is_now _pdf.pdf; Goldman Sachs, "Womenomics 4.0: Time to Walk the Talk," 2014, http:// goldmansachs.com/our-thinking/outlook/womenomics4-folder/womenomics4 -time-to-walk-the-talk.pdf.

44. Gayle Tzemach Lemmon and Becky Allen, "Japanese Companies Step Up to Support Working Mothers," Council on Foreign Relations, February 21, 2017, https://www.cfr .org/blog-post/japanese-companies-step-support-working-mothers.

45. Svati Narula, "Why Did Only 2% of New Fathers in Japan Take Paternity Leave Last Year?," World Economic Forum, January 11, 2016, https://weforum.org/agenda/2016 /01/why-did-only-2-of-new-fathers-in-japan-take-paternity-leave-last-year; Catalyst, "Women in Japan," 2015, http://catalyst.org/knowledge/women-japan.

46. 20-First, "Global Gender Balance Scorecard," 2014, http://20-first.com/wp-content /uploads/20-first-2014-Scorecard_Focus-on-Japan.pdf.

47. Matsui, 2016.

48. Randa Elnagar, "A Chance for Change: IMF Agreement to Help Bring Egypt's Economy to Its Full Potential," IMF, November 11, 2016, https://imf.org/en/News/Articles /2016/11/11/NA111116-A-Chance-For-Change-Egypt.

49. Empower Women, "The UN Secretary-General's High-Level Panel on Women's Economic Empowerment," https://www.empowerwomen.org/en/who-we-are/initiatives /sg-high-level-panel-on-womens-economic-empowerment.

50. United Nations, "Women's Empowerment Principles," http://weprinciples.org/Site /Partnership.

51. Charity Wallace, "ICYMI: A Roadmap for Promoting Women's Economic Empowerment," George W. Bush Presidential Center, 2013, http://bushcenter.org/publications /articles/2013/09/icymi-a-roadmap-for-promoting-womens-economic-empowerment .html.

52. U.S. Department of State, U.S.-Middle East Partnership Initiative, "Gender and Women's Empowerment," https://mepi.state.gov/about-mepi/gender-womens-empowerment.

53. Charlotte M. Ponticelli, "Remarks to NGO Monthly Briefing Series," U.S. Department of State, March 27, 2003, https://2001-2009.state.gov/g/wi/19423.htm.

54. The White House of President Barack Obama, "Fact Sheet: APEC Breaks Down Barriers to Women's Economic Participation," November 11, 2014, https:// obamawhitehouse.archives.gov/the-press-office/2014/11/11/fact-sheet-apec-breaks -down-barriers-women-s-economic-participation.

55. Angel Gurria, "Bringing Gender Equality to the Core of the G20 Agenda," keynote address, Women-20 official launch, September 6, 2015, https://oecd.org/g20/topics /employment-and-social-policy/bringing-gender-equality-to-the-core-of-the-g20 -agenda.htm.

56. White House, 2014.

57. Millennium Challenge Corporation, "Strengthening MCC's Gender Policy," 2011, https://mcc.gov/resources/doc/paper-2011001054301-genderintegration; Millennium Challenge Corporation, "Partnerships for Improving Gender Equality," https://mcc .gov/initiatives/initiative/gender#section-2887; see also Millennium Challenge Corporation, "Principles into Practice: Gender Equality and Poverty Reduction Through Growth," 2012, https://www.mcc.gov/resources/doc/principles-into-practice-gender -equality-and-poverty-reduction-through-grow; Millennium Challenge Corporation, "Gender in the Economy Indicator," https://mcc.gov/who-we-fund/indicator/gender -in-the-economy-indicator.

58. Millennium Challenge Corporation, "Women and Land: A Winning Combination for Economic Growth," https://mcc.gov/our-impact/story/story-women-and-land-a -winning-combination-for-economic-growth.

59. Megan O'Donnell et al., "Promoting Women's Economic Empowerment through US Foreign and Development Policy," Center for Global Development, September 2016, https://cgdev.org/publication/promoting-womens-economic-empowerment-us -foreign-development-policy.

60. Ferrant, Pesando, and Nowacka, 2014.

61. Action Aid, "Close the Gap! The Cost of Inequality in Women's Work," 2015, https://actionaid.org.uk/sites/default/files/publications/womens_rights_on-line _version_2.1.pdf.

62. Rachel Vogelstein, "Women Around the World: This Week," Council on Foreign Relations, April 28, 2017, https://www.cfr.org/blog-post/women-around-world-week-14.

63. Tavneet Suri and William Jack, "The Long-Run Poverty and Gender Impacts of Mobile Money," Science, December 2016, pp. 1288–92, http://science.sciencemag .org/content/354/6317/1288/tab-pdf.

64. Christian Gonzalez et al., "Fair Play: More Equal Laws Boost Labor Force Participation," IMF, 2015, https://imf.org/external/pubs/ft/sdn/2015/sdn1502.pdf.

65. Maritza Asencios, "Peru: Women Workers Forced into Informal Economy," Inter Press Service, December 2, 2009, http://ipsnews.net/2009/12/peru-women-workers-forced -into-informal-economy.

66. Asia-Pacific Economic Cooperation and USAID, "Women's Economic Participation in Peru," 2016, https://nathaninc.com/sites/default/files/US-ATAARI%20Peru%20 Gender%20Assessment%20(final).pdf.

67. Ibid.

68. O'Donnell et al., 2016.

69. Ibid.

70. OECD, 2014.

71. "Laboratoria," https://drive.google.com/file/d/0B8Wu6XwCFAHXSzhnWG1OOC 1OdU0/view.

72. ILO, "Report of the Conference: 19th International Conference of Labour Statisticians," October 2–11, 2013, http://ilo.org/wcmsp5/groups/public/---dgreports/---stat/documents /publication/wcms_234124.pdf.

73. Felix Velez, "Unpaid Care and Domestic Work: Valuation and Policy-Making Use," UN and INEGI, 2014, http://unstats.un.org/unsd/gender/Mexico_Nov2014/Session% 205%20Mexico%20ppt.pdf.

# About the Authors

**Gayle Tzemach Lemmon** is a journalist and senior fellow of CFR's Women and Foreign Policy program. Lemmon is the *New York Times* best-selling author of *Ashley's War: The Untold Story of a Team of Women Soldiers on the Special Ops Battlefield* and *The Dressmaker of Khair Khana*. She previously led policy efforts and worked on the emerging markets team for the global investment firm PIMCO. She worked for nearly a decade as a journalist with the ABC News political unit and *This Week with George Stephanopoulos*. A former Fulbright scholar and Robert Bosch Foundation fellow, she serves on the boards of Mercy Corps and the International Center for Research on Women and is a member of the Bretton Woods Committee. Lemmon received her bachelor's degree in journalism from the University of Missouri and her master's degree in business administration from Harvard Business School.

**Rachel Vogelstein** is senior fellow and director of CFR's Women and Foreign Policy program and professor of gender and U.S. foreign policy at Georgetown Law School. She is the author of *Ending Child Marriage* and *How Women's Participation in Conflict Prevention and Resolution Advances U.S. Interests*. From 2009 to 2012, Vogelstein was director of policy and senior advisor in the Office of Global Women's Issues within the Office of the Secretary of State at the U.S. Department of State and served as a member of the White House Council on Women and Girls. Following her tenure in government, Vogelstein was the director of women's and girls' programs in the Office of Hillary Rodham Clinton, where she oversaw the development of the No Ceilings initiative and provided guidance on domestic and global women's issues. An attorney by training, Vogelstein is a recipient of the Secretary of State's Superior Honor Award and a National Association of Women Lawyers Award, and serves on the board of trustees of the National Child Research Center.

# Advisory Committee for *Building Inclusive Economies*

Brian Atwood
*Former Chair of the OECD's Development Assistance Committee; Humphrey School of Public Affairs*

Mayra Buvinic
*Center for Global Development*

Heidi Crebo-Rediker
*Council on Foreign Relations*

Zoe Cruz
*EOZ Global*

Amanda Ellis
*Former New Zealand Head of Mission and Ambassador to the United Nations; East-West Center*

Helene Gayle
*McKinsey Social Initiative*

Markus Goldstein
*World Bank Group*

Caren Grown
*World Bank Group*

Mary Ellen Iskenderian
*Women's World Banking*

Julie Katzman
*Inter-American Development Bank*

Jeni Klugman
*Harvard Kennedy School; Georgetown Institute for Women, Peace, and Security*

Alyse Nelson
*Vital Voices*

Tom Nides
*Morgan Stanley*

Shauna Olney
*International Labor Organization*

Laura Tyson
*Haas School of Business, University of California, Berkeley*

Saadia Zahidi
*World Economic Forum*